Antigone

Roy Williams

T0348063

methuen | drama

LONDON • NEW YORK • OXFORD • NEW DELHI • SYDNEY

METHUEN DRAMA
Bloomsbury Publishing Plc
50 Bedford Square, London, WC1B 3DP, UK
1385 Broadway, New York, NY 10018, USA
29 Earlsfort Terrace, Dublin 2, Ireland

BLOOMSBURY, METHUEN DRAMA and the Methuen
Drama logo are trademarks of Bloomsbury Publishing Plc

First published in Great Britain 2014

Published in Plays For Young People Series 2021

Series design by Louise Dugdale
Cover image: Rural road going over hill
© Cultura Creative RF / Alamy Stock Photo

A catalogue record for this book is available from the British Library.

A catalog record for this book is available from the Library of Congress.

ISBN: PB: 978-1-3502-6084-9
ePDF: 978-1-3502-6085-6
eBook: 978-1-3502-6086-3

Series: Plays For Young People

Typeset by Mark Heslington Ltd, Scarborough, North Yorkshire

To find out more about our authors and books visit
www.bloomsbury.com and sign up for our newsletters.

Antigone

Characters

Antigone (**Tig**)
Esme, *sister of Tig?*
Creo, *king of Thebes?*
Eunice, *wife of Creo?*
Eamon, *son of Creo and Eunice, boyfriend of Tig*
Tyrese, *an old blind gangster*
Boy, *a young lad guiding Tyrese*
Guard, *a soldier serving Creo*
Three Soldiers (*Chorus*)

Scene One

A street in downtown Thebes.

*Blackout. A roar of traffic on the soundtrack. Lights flash overhead.
It is 2am.*

*Through the darkness a dishevelled figure shuffles into the
auditorium. He has a small torch. He shines it at us and then on the
pillars on the space. We hear traffic rumbling overhead and flashes
of light as vehicles pass above the pillars. He shines his torch into the
space. We see pillars, bins, waste and some security cameras. He
makes some sounds of displeasure at the cameras, and shines his
torch onto them. They move and focus on him.*

The following speech plays over the remaining action.

Tig   Numberless wonders terrible wonders walk the earth
but none the match for man – that great wonder crossing the
heaving grey sea, driven on by the blasts of winter, on
through breakers crashing left and right, holds his steady
course and the oldest of the gods he wears away – the earth,
the immortal, the inexhaustible – as his ploughs go back and
forth, year in, year out with the breed of stallions turning up
the furrows. Man the master, ingenious past all measure,
past all dreams, the skills within his grasp he forges on, now
to destruction, now again to greatness.

*He waves his arms and turns his back on the cameras. He looks at
the ground and finds his spot. The right spot. The exact spot. He
takes a bottle out of a plastic carrier bag he has been carrying and
drinks from it. He sits down and attempts to get himself comfortable.
He sits and looks at us. A tear rolls down his cheek.*

*He wipes it away with the back of his tattered jacket sleeve. He lies
down. A flash of light, a roar of traffic – we hear laughter / screams
and the sound of footsteps. Young people enter, a group of lads and a
couple of girls, they are laughing and joking – they stop when they
see the old guy on the floor. Is he dead? One of the girls goes over to
him and carefully checks him and puts a jacket over him . . .*

The world shifts – lights flicker and a roar of traffic and a scream – the man sits up abruptly and roars – the young people jump and scatter – the bins move, the sounds build – there is complete pandemonium – we pull back when the smoke and clatter clears.

There is a body on the ground – this time it is that of Orrin.

We see the crowd gather – the man from the floor is now watching – only this time his old coat has been removed in the melee and he is now **Creo***, king of Thebes – forced to relive the error of his actions – every night.*

People are shocked and turn around, not wanting to look anymore at the dead body or are refusing to. There are other bystanders hovering around, barely moving, **Tig** *and her sister* **Esme** *are among them.*

Creo *is joined by his soldiers who are hovering around.* **Creo** *goes to console his niece but she withdraws from him in disgust.*

Tig *watches as a kindly bystander covers the body with his jacket.*

Creo*, now accepting he must relive his past, whispers something to one of his soldiers who then whispers something in the ear of the bystander. The bystander at first protests but then removes his jacket from the body and walks away, as do several other people.*

Tig   Hey, what are you doing? Where are you going? Where are you going man? Come back.

Everyone else slowly withdraws, until **Tig** *and her sister are the only ones left.* **Tig** *removes her jacket with the intention of putting it over the dead body but is pulled away by* **Esme** *before she can do so.*

Scene Two

Thebes night club. Two days later.

Three Soldiers *enter the VIP area.*

Soldier One   Oh yes, sun shine ever so bright today, and so it should! Proud to be a fam.

Soldier Two   Proud to be of Thebes!

Soldier Three   Proud to see them Argive batty bwois run away from battle with their lives.

Soldier One   For their lives, even.

Soldier Two   Orrin think him a bad man.

Soldier Three   Orrin was a fool.

Soldier One   Him and his army.

Soldier Two   Nuttin but fools.

Soldier One   See them come?

Soldier Three   Tooled up.

Soldier One   Like you wouldn't believe.

Soldier Two   Can't believe how hard it was to dash them back.

Soldier Three   Hard? Easy more like.

Soldier One   Well I wouldn't.

Soldier Three   Well I would. We is *Thebes*. We is crew. We is fam! Hear how everyone is vibing for us?

Soldier One   I hear it.

Soldier Two   Well come, let's go! Let's get on that floor, man!

Soldier Three   Yes! Ca I want to get behind some backbone tonight!

Soldier One   You forget. Creo wants us here. We have to wait.

Soldier Two   For how long?

Soldier One   For as long.

Soldier Three   That is one brer who does not take a night off.

Soldier One   Calm yourselves, he just wants to praise us, single us out. We should be proud, problem?

Enter **Creo**. **Soldiers** *cheer.*

Creo   Yes! Here you are. Here you are! My fam! I know you all want to get out on that floor, show some moves. Do a little dance, make a little love!

Soldier One   No, fam.

Soldier Two   No way.

Soldier Three   Yeah man, we hang wid you!

Creo   You lying wretch, each and every one. No mind, point is, I have summoned you all here, yeah cos I know I can count on each and every one of you. You proved yourselves soldiers and a half when you pledged loyalty to Lais. When him dead, you never stopped in your duty when you ran with Oedipus, and when he died, you continued to lay behind his fam. Sadly, though, his two boys have gone and dashed each other out. Now, I must feel it is my place to step in, or some might say to step up! I know what people are thinking, maybe some of you are thinking the same thing. How can he call himself the boss man without being tested or nuttin? Maybe true, in fact it is true, but what is also true is that I will do what I feel is best for Thebes, you understand? I ain't got no time for anyone who thinks he or she, or anyone they might follow, is above all that. I speak when speak is needed. You won't catch me, in your days, making any deals behind the scenes, with a known enemy. Private good will not be me playing roughshod over public good, you understand? I will prove myself to all of you, with every breath. With that in mind, I have made the following decision regarding my deceased nephews. Eto' fought for his city, nothing prouder than that, and it will be my honour to bury him with full honours, no less than he deserved. Orrin on the other hand, came home to wage war, making up a whole heap of noise in the process. He turned against his fam, his city, you, all of us! No honours for him, nuttin! And I mean nuttin! His wurtless corpse is still lying there on the street as we speak and that is where I want it kept. The only thing I want messing with that body is a dawg! Are we clear on that? Let *5 O'* deal wid it when they come. No one else. I want the Feds to know, I run tings here, feel? And I want all of Thebes to know, this is what happens when you turn against your own. Thebes is my kingdom now. Say?

Soldier One   Your word is law, blud.

Creo   So, you abide?

Soldier Two   Of course, fam!

Soldier One   No need to ask.

Creo   Me yu wid?

Soldier Three   Always!

Creo   Good. Cos I want sentries on both sides of the street, watching that body, 24/7.

Soldier Three   On it, fam!

Creo   Anyone who comes near, I'll be first to know.

Soldier Three   Your word is law, fam.

Soldier Three *goes.*

Soldier Two   No fool will have the sense to go against you.

Creo   You'd be surprised. Alright enough talk, let's hit the floor, let's get drinks up here!

Soldier One   On it!

Scene Three

Ten minutes later.

Enter **Tig**, *followed by* **Esme**, *bringing in drinks and glasses. They are both in barmaid uniform.*

Tig   Just tell me summin, is it me, Esme?

Esme   Girl?

Tig   Am I the only one?

Esme   Yer losing me?

Tig   The only one girl!

Esme   One what?

Tig   That's noticed how many times we are supposed to pay for what our parents did. You name it, we've had it. Now this? Nuttin but glorified waitresses, two a we!

You should hear him. Parading himself around like he runs tings. (*Mimics* **Creo**.) '*Now, I must feel it is my place to step in.*' Our own brother ain't even cold yet.

Esme   You don't have to keep saying it.

Tig   A sign of respect, that too much to ask?

Esme   No.

Tig   But?

Esme   There is no but.

Tig   There is always a but with you.

Esme   No today, sis.

Esme *lifts up a box of ice and a bottle of champagne.*

Should we open one up?

Tig   Creo's champagne? I didn't know you were so brave, Es?

Esme   No, I meant for them.

Tig   Of course you did. What was I thinking? Nice thought though, if only for a second.

Esme   Should we open one up, or should we pour it for them when they come back, or have it ready now?

Tig   Do I look like I care either way?

Tig *takes the bottle and begins opening it.*

Esme (*protests*)   Tig!

Tig   Oh shush.

Esme   Put it down.

Tig *opens it without it flowing over.*

Tig   See it deh? It's all in the wrist. Pass two glasses over.

Esme   We shouldn't be doing this.

Tig   Don't be so boring. For Eto', and Orrin! Peace be upon them.

Tig *takes a swig. She hands the bottle to* **Esme**.

Esme (*defiant*)   No!

Tig   Yes!

Esme *takes down a huge gulp.*

Tig   Whoa! Slow down girl, this isn't a race.

Esme   I just don't want them catching us.

Tig *takes another swig.*

Tig   Nice. Maybe Creo's not so bad after all.

Esme   He might not be a bad king as well.

Tig   I said maybe Es. And that is a big maybe!

Tig *hears a track she likes.*

Oh tuuunnne! Listen to this tune!

Tig *climbs on* **Creo***'s chair and begins dancing.*

Esme   Ok, now you are just asking for trouble.

Tig   Well bring it on then, les have it.

Esme   Get down man.

Tig   Get up man!

Esme   Tig!

Tig   You're a better dancer than me, show me some moves.

Esme   I ain't getting up there.

Tig *finally climbs down.*

Tig   You are not much fun these days Esme, I hope you know that.

Esme   I'm just looking out for you.

Tig   Funny you should say.

Esme   Why? What is going through your head now?

Tig   You still wid me, girl?

Esme   You know that.

Tig   From birth to earth?

Esme   What is the matter with you? What is it?

Tig   I can't shake it, man. Creo, Orrin.

Esme   How did I know you were going to say that?

Tig   So, you don't care that one of our brothers gets treated like a soldier, the other one like a traitor.

Esme   Of course I care.

Tig   But you would rather clean tables, serve drinks for the man who put our brother down?

Esme   Orrin put himself down. You know what them two were like. One always wanted what the other one had.

Tig   It ain't right that Creo is playing the big man now. Telling everyone with ears that he will end them if anyone thinks of darking him? It's time sis.

Esme   Time for what?

Tig   To see what you are made of. You game?

Esme   What do you want me to do?

Tig Help me, that's all.

Esme To do what, girl?

Tig Cover our brother, ennit?

Esme I know I didn't hear you say that.

Tig I sad it Es.

Esme Listen to your big sister for once, just leave it.

Tig No.

Esme Could you at least, try?

Tig No.

Esme You and your nos! You love saying it, 24/7.

Tig I don't love saying it, I say it when I believe it.

Esme The police will come, let them take it.

Tig It? What you mean, it?

Esme Him, Orrin, our brother, happy?

Tig Do I look?

Esme You wear me out, man.

Tig Creo can go jump.

Esme He's the law round here.

Tig I ain't having him telling me who I should follow. I don't care if he's fam or not.

Esme What do you think Creo would do, if we went against him, think it through girl, why don't yer?

Tig Yeah, you just stand around with your apron and yer j cloth, cleaning up after him. I will just have to go and cover my brother myself, ennit.

Esme No you won't.

Tig Excuse? Yes I will.

Esme   You haven't flapped your gums to anyone else about this, have you?

Tig   No, but you can tell the whole of Thebes for all I care. if that's how you feel? Maybe you should. Imagine how they would feel, if they find out you knew all the time?

Esme   Like you summin now! Antigone, she have no fear!

Tig   It's *Tig*, and you had better believe.

Esme   But you should be, should be shaking in yer boots!

Tig   To do right by those I should do right by? You must have the wrong sister, girl.

Esme   No. You ain't doing this, you can't.

Tig   Watch me.

Esme   You can't, it's impossible.

Tig   Esme, just leave me yeah. Don't make me hate you as well.

Esme   You'll die.

Tig   You think I'm afraid?

Esme   Well go then, do what you have to! I don't know any other girl as loyal or as stupid or as mad up as you.

They exit.

Scene Four

Forty minutes later.

Soldier Three *is alone in the VIP area. He looks extremely nervous and considers helping himself to some of the drinks on offer to steady his nerves. Just as he is about to pour himself a glass and drink,* **Creo** *and the* **Soldiers** *come back from dancing on the floor, They do not seem pleased to see* **Soldier Three** *sitting there.* **Soldier Three** *quickly tries to hide the drink he poured.*

Creo   Wat diss?

Soldier Three   Sorry man, really man, I was just thirsty you know.

Soldier One   You never hear of water, dawg?

Soldier Two   Dawg, him a horse. Yer supposed to wait.

Creo   What do you want? What you doing back here?

Soldier Two   Make it good.

Soldier One   If I were you.

Soldier Three   I will.

Creo   And why is that? I thought it was all quiet out there.

Soldier Three   It was.

Creo   Was?

Soldier One   What you mean?

Creo   Yeah man, what you have for me?

Soldier Three   You know if I said I dashed to get back here, I'd be lying.

Creo   Why lie in the first place?

Soldier Three   Ca I don't want to tell you what I have to tell you.

Creo   And what is it that you have to tell me?

Soldier Three   Something that I know if you had heard from someone else, when you should by rights have heard it from me, I knew I would be in knee deep.

Creo   Well, lucky for you, you are here telling instead of someone else telling me.

Soldier Three   That's right.

Creo   I like a brer who ain't afraid to stand up.

Soldier Three   Nice.

Creo   So?

Soldier Three   So, what?

Creo   Stand up!

Soldier Three *quickly realises he has been sitting down this whole time. He jumps to his feet.*

Creo   So, you go tell me?

Soldier Three   Can I just say summin else first?

Creo   Like what?

Soldier Two   Is it me or is he shaking?

Creo   Pour him a drink.

One of the **Soldiers** *then hands* **Soldier Three** *a drink.*

Soldier Three   It weren't me.

Creo   What wasn't you?

Soldier Three   I didn't see what happened, on my life! So, don't blame me, don't lose yourself on me. I beg you!

Creo   I go lose a whole heap on you right now, if you don't speak summin.

Soldier Three   It bad.

Creo   What is?

Soldier Three   You have no idea.

Creo   Boy don't test me.

Soldier Three (*blurts it out*)   Someone covered the body.

Creo   Say that again?

Soldier Three   Orrin!

Creo   I know who it is.

Soldier Three   It must have happened tonight, cos it was lying out there, like you ordered, only a couple of hours ago, on my life, I swear!

Creo   Covered?

Soldier Three   Go out and look!

Creo   Someone has gone out and covered Orrin?

Soldier Three   Yeah.

Soldier One   Whoa!

Soldier Two   Whoa indeed!

Creo   Making me out to look like some kind a bitch?

Soldier Three   It would seem, yeah?

Soldier Two   I beg your?

Soldier Three   It would *seem* someone is trying to make you look like a bitch, like he said. Not me, obviously.

Soldier Two   You ever hear a man back pedal so?

Soldier Three   What you think, I go call your boss a bitch?

Soldier Two   Your boss too.

Soldier One   In case you forget.

Soldier Three   You two make it hard to forget.

Soldier Two   Bwoi, this brer!

Soldier One   Yeah, carry on with that mouth.

Soldier Two   See where it takes you.

Creo   Hey, excuse me, sorry to interrupt, but do you remember me, Creo? King of blood claart *Thebes*? Focus! (*To* **Soldier Three**.) Are you saying someone covered him up?

Soldier Three   With his own coat, yes.

Creo   For sure?

Soldier Three   For sure.

Creo   Well that is it. That is truly it. After all that I said, someone out there have the front to . . . For real gents, this is a brer, one brave brer that I want to meet. Who would dare?

Soldier Three   I don't know, but they were quiet.

Creo   Quiet?

Soldier Three   Whoever it was, they did it right from under our noses. No sound, no sight, we couldn't believe our eyes! We just started yelling at each other, who could have missed this, how could no one see that, you know.

Creo   No? No, I don't know. How could I blasted well know?

Soldier Three   Right, now yer vex wid me.

Creo   You think?

Soldier Three   I didn't even want to come.

Creo   But you did.

Soldier Three   Only cos I lost the bet.

Soldier Two   What?

Soldier Three   What, what?

Soldier One   What was the bet?

Soldier Three *takes his phone out, shows them a picture.*

Soldier Three   See?

Soldier Two   Seeing what?

Soldier Three   Two blackbirds sitting on a tree, in the park. Byline say *'Attempted Murder'*. The other sentries bet me this trip, that I wouldn't get it.

Soldier Two   I don't get it.

Soldier Three   There was me thinking you had smarts.

Soldier Two Keep running off that mouth, you will see how smart I am.

You know what it means then, big man?

Soldier Three If I knew, it wouldn't be me, standing here, now would it?

Soldier Two I go kick start your head in a minute.

Soldier Three I didn't want to be here, you think I wanted to be the one who tells you? You mad?

Soldier Two *Blackbirds? Attempted murder.*

Soldier Three I still don't get it.

Soldier One How about some licks, you wanna get a couple of those?

Soldier Two *and* **Soldier Three** *get out their phones so they can go on Google search engine.*

Soldier One Creo?

Creo I hear you.

Soldier One Some weird vibes here man.

Creo Don't even start wid that.

Soldier One Start what?

Creo Don't bring 'this is the work of the gods' anywhere near this. So, someone close to home it would seem, don't seem to like what I am going on with. It wouldn't surprise me if they bribed my sentries to look the other way.

Soldier Three Say?

Creo Anything you want to tell me?

Soldier Three Say what? Creo man, I roll with you.

Creo So, that would be a no then?

Soldier Three No, I mean yes, yes, a definite yes!

Soldier One   Look 'pon him, he's meeting himself coming back.

Soldier Three   I'm so done.

Soldier One   Really done?

Soldier Three   Like you wouldn't believe. Nothing else.

Creo   Sure about that?

Soldier Three   Better believe!

Creo   Find out who it was, is what I say. Find them, then bring them to me. Ca if you don't, I'm gonna string you up, you understand? I need someone to blame, so it might as well be you. Then you will see if money is worth what you had to do to get it.

Soldier Three   Can I just say something please?

Creo   Just as long as you make it worth my while, ca your mouth is starting to annoy me a little here.

Soldier Three   Cos of my voice, or the truth?

Creo   Is this you trying to psych me?

Soldier Three   I'm just a soldier, I don't know how you feel.

Creo   Answer for everything.

Soldier Three   So I have been told.

Creo   Come out of my range.

Soldier Three   Look, I know I can go on sometimes.

Creo   Sometimes?

Soldier Three   But I know I ain't done nuttin wrong here.

Creo   Until now.

Soldier Three   You're jumping to conclusions here, big time.

Creo   You don't bring me the one who did this, I'll be jumping on you. I'm going for a slash. I see you again, you had better have summin for me.

Creo *exits.*

Soldier Three (*mutters*)   No you won't, cos I'm gone.

Soldier One   Yeah you are. Right now.

Soldier Three *goes.*

Soldier One *sees the other soldier still on his phone.*

Soldier Two   I can't get a signal in here. Two blackbirds? In a tree?

Attempted murder? I hate it when I get things like this, this is going to bug me all night.

Soldier One   You still on with that, seriously?

Soldier Two   Well, what else is there, then?

Soldier One   Your ears gone deaf for the last five minutes? You don't know summin's going down?

Soldier Two   And here it comes. Him and his chat about gods.

Soldier One   Hey, in case you forget.

The **Soldier** *points to the security cameras above.*

Soldier Two   Those things ain't even working.

Soldier One   I saw them move when I come in here.

Soldier Two   You didn't see shit.

Soldier One   Just because you don't believe it, that don't make it so. The gods don't allow nuttin if it weren't to be. Someone covering up Orrin, weren't meant to be.

Soldier Two   But someone did it though.

Soldier One   That's what bothers me. Maybe it was.

Soldier Two   Was what?

Soldier One   Meant to be, you fool!

Soldier Two   You think the gods are moving against Creo?

Soldier One   If they are, the last place I want to be is between them.

Soldier Two   Don't let Creo hear you. Yer lucky he ain't come out.

What's he pissing in there, a river?

Soldier One   He's taking a dump, fool.

Soldier Two   Why didn't he say?

Soldier One   No one says.

Soldier Two   A signal, one bar. (*Types.*) Blackbird, attempted murder. Man I lost the bar now.

Soldier One   I had a feeling, you know. This was too easy.

Soldier Two   You carry on like the war ain't finished. Some fool trying his luck that is all.

Soldier One   Creo is the one trying his luck.

Soldier Two   You a step away from calling him a fool you know.

Soldier One   No, I'm saying he always likes to push it a little. If you really think about it, he didn't need to shame Orrin, side with Eto' like that. It was a little uncalled, don't you think? Brothers business, let them deal wid it.

Soldier Two   The two a them were running *Thebes* into the ground. You know that. Creo running tings now.

Soldier One   That's what we think.

Soldier Two   Get on. Or get off.

Soldier One   I'm on, as long as the gods wish it.

Soldier Two   You and your gods! Don't I have a say? Don't we all ever have a say?

Soldier One   Of course you do. Unwind yourself. We is fam, I'm just saying.

Soldier Two   Well don't. I chose to roll with Creo. That's where I come out. End of. I can't believe how slow this phone is. All I got was *Raven*. What's that?

Soldier One   A blackbird, you fool.

Soldier Two   I still don't get it.

Soldier One (*shakes his head; he gets it*)   Take your time, blud.

Soldier Three *enters with* **Tig**.

Soldier Three   See it deh? See what I bring for you?

The **Soldiers** *laugh.*

Soldier Three   What?

Soldier One   Nuttin.

Soldier Three   Don't even think of darking me now?

Soldier One   Thought never crossed.

Soldier Two   That is one big fish you catch there.

Soldier Three   Believe that.

Soldier One   But if I was you, I'd fling it back.

Soldier Three   Excuse?

Soldier Two   Take her back to the bar downstairs. Right now.

Soldier One   Before you find yourself.

Soldier Two   In a world of hurt.

Soldier Three   I didn't find her at the bar.

Soldier Two   Fine then!

Soldier One   Put her back.

Soldier Two   Wherever you did find her.

Soldier One   Before Creo lay eyes.

Soldier Two   And dead's you where you stand.

Soldier Three   Ok, I don't think you boys understand. This is what Creo wants.

Soldier Two   How can this be what Creo wants?

Soldier One   You don't know who this is yungsta?

Soldier Three   Tig, the inbreed.

Tig   Say what?

Soldier Three   Who I catch.

Soldier One   To do what?

Soldier Two   To go down on you?

Soldier One   Brudda, I could throw a stone down to the dance floor, hit a gal who could do that fer you.

Soldier Three   Are you boys ever going to let me finish what I am trying to say . . .

Tig (*cutting in*)   In his arse boring, going around two blocks, on his hands and knees like a bitch kind of way, is that it was me.

Soldier One   What was you?

Tig   I covered Orrin.

Soldier Three   You want look?

Soldier Three *shows the soldiers video footage from his phone of* **Tig** *covering the body of her dead brother.*

Soldier One   Tig?

Tig   Yeah, that's me.

Soldier One   Girl. What are you doing?

Soldier Three   We caught her in the act. Just now man.

Soldier One   Was I chatting to you? Speak, girl.

Soldier Three   Got her all on *HD*, nuttin finer than that.

Soldier Two   Is this you letting her speak? Yes or no? Tig?
Come on girl, what is this?

Creo *enters*.

Creo   Yes, tell me what this?

Soldier Three   You know what, I swore I would never
bring myself back here, not unless we got the one you are
looking for so hear what?

Creo   What?

Soldier Three   The one you are looking for, her that!

Creo   Her?

Soldier Three   We caught her red-handed a minute ago,
trying to cover her brother, the man you said was not to be
approached, not to be touched in fact.

Creo   I know what I said, I was there.

Soldier Three   Just thought I'd remind you.

Soldier One   Don't do it.

Soldier Three   What?

Soldier Two   Don't get renk.

Creo   Why you bring her here?

Soldier Three   She was trying to cover him again. You
couldn't have that, you said.

Creo   Do you have any idea what you are telling me
right now?

Soldier Three   Yeah, but this time I saw her with my own
eyes. Even filmed it, so to be sure.

Creo   Tell me.

Soldier Three   Show!

Creo   Tell me what you saw?

Soldier Three   It's just after I left here. I weren't gonna forget what you said about stringing me up, make it look like I was the one who did it, if I didn't find out who it really was so I went back to my post, body starting to smell, Creo, no word of a lie, it stinks! Anyhow. I had my phone ready to record, and well, see for yourself, large as life I'm telling you. See her now, kneeling down beside the body, calling us all kind of names and that. Then she does it again.

Creo   I got eyes you know.

Soldier Three   I did good, yeah? She didn't deny it, not for a second. I don't think this girl is afraid of anything, even dying, well better her than me.

Creo   Tig? Look me in the eye, girl!

Tig   Don't ask me if it's true. You know what you saw.

Creo (*to* **Soldier Three**) You just got a touch.

Soldier Two   Believe.

Creo   Correct me if I am wrong, but you did hear me say that your brother's body was not to be touched, you did hear me say that?

Tig   There ain't no one who didn't hear that.

Creo   But you chose to do it anyway?

Tig   Yes.

Creo   Defy me?

Tig   Yes.

Creo   I let you live?

Tig   Yes.

Creo   I give you a job in my club?

Tig   Yes, yes, yes, dayz man!

Creo   And this is how you repay me?

Tig   For what I hope is the last time . . .

Creo   What am I supposed to do wid you?

Tig   I had to choose, innit?

Creo   Yeah, choose what?

Tig   Between you and what is right.

Creo   So you chose?

Tig   I don't care how much of a big man you think you are, Creo.

Soldier Two   Oh Gosh!

Creo   Think? She say think?

Soldier One   I'm afraid she did, man.

Tig   I couldn't leave him Creo. I couldn't leave my own brother like that. I couldn't make him or me suffer like that. This way, the only way, makes sure my brother's at peace, yeah? At peace! Which we all are, at least we are supposed to be. I know you what you're thinking, that I'm stupid or summin. You think that's going to worry me?

Creo   It should be.

Tig   When you are acting more stupid than both of us put together. I don't think.

Creo   You come just like yer dad, and his mother, or should I say wife?

Soldier Three (*chuckles*)   Cold.

Soldier Two   But true.

Creo   No wonder you are all mad up in the head. Yer tough girl I give you that. But who tell you to big yourself up like that, who tell you had the right? Are you the man and I am the woman or summin? You think I won't dead you, you and your sister?

Tig   Leave her!

Creo   Leave her?

Soldier Two   You don't give orders, Tig.

Tig   It was me, not Esme.

Creo   I don't care. (*To* **Soldier Three**.) Go bring her!

Soldier Three   Where she at?

Creo   I don't know! Find out.

Soldier Three   Alright!

Soldier One   Bar downstairs yer ejut!

Creo   If she ain't there, just go follow the sounds of her crying! Gal love to cry.

Soldier Three *goes.*

Creo (*sees* **Tig**'s *concerned face*)   What? You say jump, Esme says how high, it's been that way ever since she was born, don't tek me fer a fool.

Tig   What you want now?

Creo   To see you pay, so you learn, nuff said.

Tig   Well kill me then, hurry it up. Ca I'm done with chatting to you. You know if people weren't so afraid, they'd be in here, praising me for what I have done. But it seems only boys who think they are big men are allowed to talk in here.

Creo   You honestly believe no one would think yer mad for what you did?

Tig   Yeah I do!

Creo   Well I don't.

Tig   I don't business!

Creo   People follow me. Whole of *Thebes*, man.

Tig   Only cos they fear you. Well I don't.

Creo   Lie!

Tig   Not if it means I can't give my dead brother his due.

Creo   Eto' was your brother as well in case you forget?

Tig   Of course I haven't.

Creo   But you want to shit on his memory?

Tig   That's not what he would think.

Creo   Yes he would. That is exactly what he would think. I rolled with Eto'. He and I did some serious grafting together.

Tig   I know that.

Creo   I knew him as well as you, if not more so, in fact. As much as you choose to cover his wurtless brother.

Tig   But he was still his brother.

Creo   A brother who moved against him. Against his own fam.

Tig   That don't mean.

Creo   Yes Tig, it does, it does mean!

Tig   You think you know it all as much as you have it all, don't you?

Creo   Traitors die, end of.

Tig   We all die. End of!

Creo   This is great, this is beautiful, some low-down sket, some inbreed and a half, who thinks she has jokes, is giving me back chat! Wa gwan wid that?

Soldier Three *returns with* **Esme**.

Soldier Three   Here she is. I found her in the ladies. See her eyes? All red from crying, nonstop. You were not wrong.

Creo   I bring you two into my crib, I give you work in my club. And this is how you behave? This is what you choose to go on with? Esme? You got summin to say, you deny what's going on? Esme? Hello? Come on girl, enough, dry your eyes. You heard what I said. School me.

Esme   No, I don't deny it. I told her to do it.

Tig   Es?

Esme   I did.

Tig   No she didn't.

Esme   Girl?

Tig   She's lying. Can't you see?

Esme   Tig man!

Tig   I won't let you.

Esme   You need me though. You can't go through this by yourself. What about me?

Tig   It's not about you.

Esme   I care about you.

Tig   If you really cared. You would do more than talk.

Esme   Why are you being so mean? I'm your sister. I would be willing to die for you, why don't you let me?

Tig   You don't have to, that is what I am saying, He's got me, that's enough.

Esme   How am I supposed to carry on without you? I want to help.

Tig   Save yourself. If you want to help me, do that. I'm not going to envy you your life. Why should I?

Esme   You go, I go.

Tig   You don't want to, not really.

Esme   You go, I go, girl.

Creo (*aside*)   Look at them. Hear them chat so. One's lost her mind, the other never had one to begin with. Was that it? Have you both finished now?

Esme   Everything's mad up, everyone's gone mad lately.

Soldier Two   Wid yer genes, I ain't surprised.

Creo   What's mad is you siding with your sister.

Esme   How do you expect me to go on living without her?

Creo   Like she said, she's already dead, but you ain't.

Esme   Why are you chatting to me like this? We is fam! She's going out with your son, man!

Creo   There's always another sket. You think I would ever let her near him now?

Esme   Eamon loves her though. He'd go mad if he saw what you were doing.

Creo   I'm done hearing your noise.

Soldier One   Creo, hold up a minute.

Creo   For what?

Soldier One   Hate to say . . .

Creo   But you're going to?

Soldier One   She might have a point that's all I'm saying.

Creo   What's your point?

Soldier One   Are you really going to make your boy suffer like this?

Creo   You chat as if it is my fault. Or is this your precious gods talking? (*Points at the cameras.*) Them two are the ones who are darking me, stepping out like this.

Soldier One   So, she go die?

Creo   Maybe! I don't know yet. Come on, let's move! Get these two out of my sight, (*points to* **Tig**) put this one in the cellar (*points to* **Esme**) and this one, take her home, and keep them there until I know what to do with them.

Tig *and* **Esme** *are led out by* **Soldier Three**.

Creo   Is this a club or what? I want to dance. What are you staring at?

Soldier One   Nuttin man.

Creo   I thought you all wanted to get behind some backbone? Well come on, dance floor is this way!

The **Soldiers** *follow* **Creo** *onto the dance floor.*

Scene Five

An hour later.

Eunice *and her son* **Eamon** *enter the VIP area.*

Eunice   So, are you going to tell me?

Eamon   Tell you what?

Eunice   You don't have to feel shame.

Eamon   'bout what?

Eunice   I think it's nice.

Eamon   Don't know what this woman is chatting about.

Eunice *cannot believe* **Eamon** *has said that.*

Eunice   Eh, eh!

Eamon   What, you gonna start now?

Eunice   Yes, bwoi, up and down on your head!

Eamon   Move!

Eunice   Eamon!

Eamon   Why you love to mek up noise?

Eunice   What kind of way is that to speak?

Eamon (*sarcastic*)   No way?

Eunice   I'm curious. I want to know who the girl is that is dating my handsome son.

Eamon   She's just a girl, she ain't nuttin.

Eunice   Didn't look like 'nuttin'! You were eating each other.

Eamon   That was yesterday.

Eunice   But you are sweet with her? Yes? Eamon?

Eamon   I chucked her.

Eunice   That is not what I asked, boy. Well at least tell me her name?

Eamon   Why?

Eunice   I'm nosey, can't you tell? Eamon?

Eamon   Daniela.

Eunice   And where does this Daniela live?

Eamon   In *Old Thebes*.

Eunice   *Old Thebes*?

Eamon   She ain't like that.

Eunice   Please tell me she ain't no skank.

Eamon   No.

Eunice   I can't be dealing with no skank.

Eamon   She ain't no skank, Mum.

Eunice   It's skank city in *Old Thebes*.

Eamon   You're from *Old Thebes*.

Eunice   That's how I know.

Eamon   Are you ever going to listen to me?

Eunice   But she is in your year, yeah?

Eamon   Yes, she's in my year. You wanna know her mobile number as well? How about her email address? Star sign, about her dress size?

Eunice   How about I knock yer arse into the middle of next week?

Eamon   Don't tell anyone yeah.

Eunice   Who am I going to tell, Eamon?

Eamon   Dad, for one?

Eunice   Would that be so bad? He won't mind. He'll be relieved, come to think of it.

Eamon   Why?

Eunice   Why do you think?

Eamon   Antigone?

Eunice   That girl is bad news.

Eamon   Why can't you ever say her name, Mum?

Eunice   No mind what her name is. Just tell me you are over her.

Eamon   Yeah, I'm over her. Over and out.

Eunice   Well that's good to hear, that will make this easier.

Eamon   Say?

Eunice   She's gone too far. She's defied your father publicly this time.

Eamon   What did she do?

Eunice   He can't have that.

Eamon   What did she do?

Eunice   Over and out, isn't it?

Eamon   You go tell me?

Eunice   I must look like a right fool to you. Your father gave orders, Orrin's body was not to be touched.

Eamon   Well?

Eunice   Well, what you think?

Eamon   It's her brother.

Eunice   She is mad up in the head, what you expect from an inbreeding little . . .

Eamon   Yeah, alright, I know you hate her, the whole of *Thebes* knows, happy?

Eunice   Happy? True say, you don't know your mother. Now, are you going to let this go or what? Eamon, look at me!

Eamon *looks at her, he is fighting back the tears.*

Eunice   Boy, this can't go on, you know. You're going to be king one day, you understand . . .

Eamon   I need some air.

Eunice   You can't go, your father is expecting you.

Eamon   Just let me go, Mum.

Eamon *dashes out.*

Eamon   Yeah go run, that go help!

A **Soldier** *and* **Soldier Three** *enter.* **Soldier Three** *has his phone.*

Soldier Two   Told you, I can't get a good signal up here.

Soldier Three   No, but I can. (*Reads from screen.*) See it deh? Blackbird, raven, crow?

Soldier Two   So?

Soldier Three   Which is it *Raven, Crow?* Attempted murder, *Raven, crow? Crow, raven?*

They finally notice **Eunice** *is sitting there.*

Soldier Three   Oh, sorry yeah.

Soldier Two   We didn't know.

Soldier Three   Can I get you summin?

Eunice   The inbreed, Where?

Soldier Two   Downstairs. Cellar.

Eunice *leaves without saying another word.*

Scene Six

The club cellar. Five minutes later.

Tig *is facing* **Eunice** *in the cellar.*

Eunice   I do not have long.

Tig   That makes two of us. Is Eamon alright? Does he know I'm here?

Eunice   I don't keep secrets from my son.

Tig   I know that. I wouldn't ask you to. I just want to be the one that tells him, to explain why I am doing this.

Eunice   Why you went behind his father, defied him in front of the entire city?

Tig   Yeah, that!

Eunice   You look nervous.

Tig   I'm going to die.

Eunice   You don't know that.

Tig   This is Creo we are talking about.

Eunice   Just say you're sorry.

Tig   I don't know if I can do that.

Eunice   Then you are right, you are going to die.

Tig   I said I don't know.

Eunice   What is it that you are trying to tell me?

Tig   Did Eamon tell you, that I was going back to school?

Eunice   No.

Tig   He kept going at me about going back. You got a son who don't like to shut up yer nuh. On and on about me having a brain, and it's time I used it. Only going back to school to keep him quiet.

Eunice   You should be going back because it is what you want.

Tig   It is what I want.

Eunice   I'm sorry?

Tig   It might be what I want.

Eunice   How is that possible?

Tig   Anything is possible.

Eunice   So, are you willing to renounce your brother? Beg my husband for forgiveness?

Tig   Maybe.

Eunice   No.

Tig   No? Why? Why no?

Eunice   You are twisting yourself up inside at the very thought.

Tig   And I bet you love that. All I am asking for is a chance.

Eunice   Another one?

Tig   You see! You're doing it again.

Eunice   Keep your voice down.

Tig   Every time I reach out to you, you slap me down.

Eunice   I am not doing anything of the kind.

Tig   What do you expect me to do?

Eunice   You shouldn't be so angry all of the time.

Tig   If you accept me, I will renounce my brother yeah, I will renounce him as the stupid mad up idiot that he was. I will beg Creo for forgiveness if that's what you want.

Eunice   More games.

Tig   It is not a game.

Eunice   I don't want you to renounce.

Tig   You don't?

Eunice   I want you to die.

Tig   Say what?

Eunice   I'm sorry Tig, I am so sorry, but this, what we are doing right now, you trying to be ever so nice . . .

Tig   What is so wrong with me doing that?

Eunice   Because you cannot stand the sight of me. You never have. I cannot say I have liked you much either.

Tig   Why are you doing this to me, why can't you give me a chance? Can't you see how hard this is?

Eunice   Because it's wrong, you and my son, It's wrong. And I think you know that.

Tig   S'right. Dass cool.

Eunice   Good.

Tig   I was going back to school you know, I was. I really was. Until my brothers went all mad up at each other, them and their stupid war. Dragging me down like they always do.

Eunice   It's where you belong, and don't forget my man having to come in and clean up their mess.

Tig   Alright, fine. Point is, you don't know me as well as you think. None of you do.

Eunice   Right, ok.

Tig   Ok?

Eunice   This is pointless. Creo is going to dead you, you will never see my son again.

Tig   I was trying to be nice, that is possible you know?

Eunice   For the likes of you?

Tig   Yes, for the likes of me! I honestly thought, you and me could be tight.

Eunice   Goodbye, Tig.

Tig   Bitch don't turn yer back on me! Yu think yer all that now, darking me? Who are you, who exactly are you? You had nothing til you laid eyes on Creo, till he blinged you up. Look me in the eye, tell me I'm wrong I dare you.

Eunice (*looks her in the eye*)   You are not wrong. I know where I came from. I used to see your dad, strutting himself around Thebes like he owned it, with his secrets, with his lies, his nastiness! I grew up thinking, who is he to be barking orders at us, telling us how to live, when he himself was crazier than a rabid dog! Who are his sons? Who are you? I knew you would do something like this. There was no way they (*points to the cameras*) would allow you to be with my son.

Tig   The gods had nothing to do with it. I'm responsible for my actions.

Eunice   You're more sick than your father.

Tig   Don't tell me to break up with Eamon, like I'm troubling him. You want tell him, he's the one who was always troubling me.

Eunice   So push him away.

Tig   Mek me. He'll grieve for me, you know that. He will never love another. He will never give Creo a grandson.

Eunice   Do you want money?

Tig   Money?

Eunice   Are you shaking me down, is that what it is?

Tig   You ought to know, you are the one from *Old Thebes!*

Eunice   And yet I am here, and you are there, now answer the question. If I give you money, can you escape, can you leave Thebes and never return?

Tig   Look where I am.

Eunice   Prisoners have been known to escape. You will be surprised at what I can arrange.

Tig   No.

Eunice   Girl, don't play me.

Tig   I am not playing you! I don't want your money.

Eunice   I'm serious about this.

Tig   Believe yer serious. You really hate me that much?

Eamon ain't happy you know. I can make him happy, I can love him, why can't you believe that?

Eunice *goes to leave.*

Yeah, go on, say it nasty dirty Tig with her incestuous blood, with a mad king for a dad! I've heard worse you know! What she do, go corrupt yer sweet-looking boy. Your precious straight As church going boy! You think I want something bad to happen to him? I will die first before I let anything bad happen to him. I will die if anything bad did happen to him. Why can't you see that? What is your problem man?

Eunice *lunges at* **Tig**, *grabbing her by the throat.*

Eunice   You are going to die, and nothing bad will happen to him.

Eunice *releases* **Tig**.

You will not see him. You will die without seeing him.

Scene Seven

Ten minutes later.

The **Soldiers** *come back into the VIP area.*

Soldier One   This don't feel right somehow.

Soldier Two   How so?

Soldier One   If it was just about Tig turning against Creo, fair enough.

Soldier Three   Which she has.

Soldier Two   Like her wurtless brother.

Soldier Three   Remember that.

Soldier Three *pours himself a drink.*

Soldier One   Yeah, I remember, *Sentry!*

Soldier One *snatches the drink off him.*

Soldier Two   She just needs to stop her noise. That is all.

Soldier Three   Creo may punish.

Soldier Two   But he'll forgive. Done deal.

Soldier One   I don't know.

Soldier Two   You don't know much.

Soldier Three   What do you know?

Soldier One   It's what I feel.

Soldier Three   Which is?

Soldier One   She's mad up in the head like her dad. She's going to end up like him, same way. That ain't her fault, it wouldn't hurt him to show a little leniency, that's all.

Soldier Two   *Crow Raven, attempted murder* what do you say?

Soldier One   I think you are a couple of chiefs, who are too stupid to live. You still don't get it? It's screaming at yer!

Soldier Two   Hey, look pon.

Eamon *enters. Led in by* **Creo.**

Soldier Two   Let's see where this goes?

Creo   See what I find here. My boy, come see me. About time! Now that is what I am talking. You know my boy Eamon ennit?

Soldier Two   Yeah, fam.

Soldier One   We know him.

Creo   Good. Cos one day, you'll be working for him. That is what a kingdom is about, from father to son. Where you have been?

Eamon   Around, outside, needed some air.

Creo   You're my son. The rightful heir to *Thebes!* You don't *need* anything. You want summin, it's yours. Just tek it. So, what can I do for you boy? Speak up, we're all friends here, don't be shy. What's up with you?

Eamon   Nuttin.

Creo   Like yer afraid of me.

Eamon   I'm not.

Creo   Good, cos I've got things to say. About your future.

Eamon Yeah?

Creo I take you've heard about Tig? What's going down, her and her foolishness!

Eamon Yeah.

Creo That's it, yeah?

Eamon I heard Dad, what's up?

Creo You know I had to do something, that I couldn't just let it lie.

Eamon Yeah, I know.

Creo She one ain't giving me much choice here.

Eamon I know that.

Creo Well?

Eamon Well?

Creo Is there an echo in here, or maybe you can't hear, do you want me to tell them to turn the music down?

Eamon Dad, it's a club.

Creo My club. Your club. And we will do what we want in it. So, how do you feel about what's going on with Tig? Speak your mind, boy?

Eamon Yer my dad, innit?

Creo I know that, what else?

Eamon You must know what you are doing?

Creo And? What else?

Eamon I trust your judgment. If you're happy, I'm happy.

Creo Say it.

Eamon You want me to dash her, say the word, and she's gone. History!

Creo   Thass it! Deh you go! Those are the words every father wants to hear, what a man should always want from his own. Side by side, no question, no doubt! Not a trace! A boy who will fight fer him *papa*! For real! I have to say you had me worried there for a minute though.

Eamon   How so?

Creo   The look you were giving me when you came on, same look your mother used to give when I was out at nights grafting. But nuh mind that. I'm just glad that you haven't let that crazy bitch gal turn yer head fully around. Trust me on this, hear me.

Eamon   I hear you.

Creo   There is nothing, and I mean nothing worse than spending your entire life with the wrong woman! Tig was wrong, you know that. Cold like her mum. Mad up in the head, like her dad. I bet she ain't even free it up for you, yet? Be honest!

Eamon   Dad, man?

Creo   Right or wrong?

Eamon   Look.

Creo   Don't worry, I know, I can tell. I can always see through a boy who ain't getting any. Just dash it, like you said. Gal is nuttin but a traitor to you, me, to us all, fam!

Eamon   Dad?

Creo   If I don't dead her like me say, I go look bad! I can't have that. In some eyes, I'd be a traitor as well. I can't have that.

Eamon   Even though she's fam?

Creo   Especially cos she's fam! If I let her off, let this pass, what does it say about me? Who's gonna listen to me, respect me, fear me? The people have to know that I don't play, for anyone! That I am obeyed, no matter what. A man who knows how to obey, also knows how to command. Cos he will stand his ground on the battlefield, and will not move an inch, for anyone! Without that, we've got madness going on. And that ain't going to happen yeah, not on my watch. We have to man up, two a we, don't take shit from anyone, especially some wurtless sket! You don't want to go around, saying you got bitch slapped?

Soldier Two   Word dat.

Eamon   Dad, I hear what yer saying, you know that.

Creo   Am glad to hear.

Eamon   Yer looking out for me, much appreciated.

Creo   Is it me, or is there some *buts* coming? What have I said to you, over and over about speaking your mind? Get to it boy.

Eamon   I know where you are coming from.

Creo   Today, son, not tomorrow.

Eamon   You don't think there is another way of looking at this?

Creo   Say? Explain yourself.

Eamon   Dad, you can't hear what peeps are saying, but I can.

Creo   And what are they saying, boy?

Eamon   What they think.

Creo   Which is what?

Eamon   That you shouldn't be doing this.

Creo   Oh, is it now?

Eamon   A whole heap of chat, Dad.

Creo   Go on.

Eamon   That, maybe she should be praised for what she did, standing up for what she thinks is right. It's her brother, Dad, she want to do right for him, that is all, what's the harm?

Creo   Harm?

Eamon   Don't go off, yeah.

Creo   Who says I'm going off?

Eamon   No one.

Creo   Any one of you saying I'm going off?

Soldier Two   No fam!

Soldier Three   Not me.

Creo   You know why I'm not going off?

Soldier One   No, why.

Creo   Because you will know when I am going off. For real.

Eamon   Dad, you mean more to me than anyone. Yeah.

Creo   Yer coulda fooled.

Eamon   Yer admired, that fills me up with nuttin but pride. Pride still that I'm yer son, yer blood. I'm just asking you to listen, like yer listening to me now, and that's good.

Creo   Is it me, or are you playing me?

Eamon   No, no way.

Creo   It sounds like you are playing me.

Eamon   Would I do that?

Creo   You tell me.

Eamon   Dad, I'm not playing you.

Creo   I'm glad to hear. So what? Finish yer point.

Eamon   It won't kill you to hear the people out you know? Just to show you can. You told me once any man who shouts how smarter he is than someone else, always fall on his face, without a doubt. But a smart man listens, he bends. People out there are tired, Dad, They are tired of wars, the fighting.

Creo   But there is no war.

Eamon   Only until the next fool wants to step into your endz.

Creo   Then I will deal with him, whoever he is.

Eamon   Why do you have to?

Creo   Because I'm Creo, because I'm king!

Eamon   Dad, I know yer angry, but you can afford to get past that. To show that you can learn from others. Don't you think?

Soldier One   Word dat. You both speak the trut.

Creo   Is who are you?

Soldier One   No one!

Creo   Who tell you to speak?

Soldier One   Sorry, fam.

Creo   Well keep yer tail quiet then. Telling me I should let myself be schooled by a bwoi!

Eamon   Alright, I'm a boy.

Creo   A foolish wurtless boy! I go ask yer mudda again, if yer really mine, cos this can't be happening to me right now, what it is that I am hearing!

Eamon   Does it matter how old I am? Shouldn't it matter what I say? The people want justice. Tig deserves justice.

Creo   She had it.

Eamon   Nuh man.

Creo   Nuh man?

Eamon   What you giving her, ain't justice.

Creo   Then what is it? If ain't justice, if I ain't the law, what am I? What a I good for? You telling me to let her do what she likes, break the law, whenever she feel?

Eamon   She didn't break the law.

Creo   She heard what I said. About her brother. That ain't right.

Eamon   According to you.

Creo   Who else?

Eamon   Them out there, the people.

Creo   Them? You want me to let them decide?

Eamon   Who's the boy now, Dad?

Creo   You want them to tell me how I should rule?

Eamon   It's the way it should be.

Creo   The people you love so much, don't know shit. They will do whatever people in power tell them to do, whether they realize it or not. I'm the way it should be. I am the way it has always been.

Eamon   A man who thinks only one way ain't got nuttin.

Creo   A man who sides wid a woman, ain't nuttin but a pussy! A boy, who come like a gal. Who does that sound like to you? You don't know? (*To* **Soldiers**.) Pass him a mirror.

Eamon   I'm just trying to help you.

Creo   By darking me like this? My own son?

Eamon   Yer making a mistake here.

Creo   I uphold the law round here, how is that a mistake?

Eamon   Cos yer breaking the most natural one there is, man!

Creo   Damn, that girl had got you well under! *'The most natural one there is.'* Hear him!

Eamon   She's just got me thinking, that's all.

Creo   Pussy boy, move!

Eamon   For the first time in my life.

Creo   I say move yourself!

Eamon   It's not just you that chat!

Creo   Crying to me on her behalf, what wrong wid you?

Eamon   No Dad, I cry for you.

Creo   I'll dead you first before I ever see that.

Eamon   For me, for everyone. If you carry on like this.

Creo   So all that talk about you being with me side by side, was nuttin but chat? Are you gonna tell me you still wanna see her? Speak boy?

Eamon   Yes.

Creo   Good luck with that, I dead her, right now!

Eamon   You will have to dead me next!

Creo   So my boy think him man, threatening him papa!

Eamon   I'm just saying.

Creo   You been saying a lot, more than I ever heard from you on my life in fact. Normally, I'd be impressed but you chatting back to me, the way you have been, I can't have.

Eamon   Yer lucky yer my dad.

Creo   Lucky?

Eamon   Cos I would a called you a whole heap of names, the minute I stepped in here.

Creo   Well say them, get them off man, now! Lay them on me cos as of now yer no son of mine.

Soldier One   Hey Creo, man.

Creo   Official. I don't want to hear another word from you. (*To* **Eamon**.) Following some yat around like some dog, bring me shame!

Eamon   Can't say nuttin to you, can I?

Creo   No. It break my heart to say, but there's nuttin I want to hear.

Eamon   The way you like it.

Creo   You are done now.

Eamon   Now and forever.

Creo (*to* **Soldier Three**) Drag that little wurtless bitch out here, now me say! I go dead her, right here in front of him. Bring an end to this foolishness.

Eamon   Don't think you will ever see me again, if you do. Only some crazy arsed crack head from *Old Thebes* will want look at you now.

Creo   Well step then! On your way!

Eamon *exits*.

Creo (*to* **Soldier One**) What? You wat speak as well? Let's hear it.

Soldier One   You sure you want him going off like that? Boy is liable to do anything right now.

Creo   What can he do? Him still a boy, he can't hurt me. And he can't save her, he's mad if he thinks I'm gonna let her live, that I go low dat, that he thinks he can just walk away from Thebes. Cos come the day when I pass on, he will rule, there's nothing else. He can cry all he likes but that, my friend, go happen, so listen: if I kill that little bitch off now, he will see, for real, that I don't play, come to his senses and get on his knees for me, people of Thebes as well, how about that? Make it a good one for her. A special!

Soldier One   How?

Creo   She want cover her brother, I say we cover her, in the darkest hole we can find for her.

Soldier One   What, alive?

Creo   My brother! True say, you know yer king! Drive her to the quarry. Dig the deepest hole you can, give her food and water, to take down with her a whole heap. Then let me hear some say, I go kill her. Let her make up noise about me, Creo this, Creo that! Let her pray to God to get her out. Maybe. Just maybe she will beg me not to throw her arse in there, that maybe she'll realise she could care more about the living than the wurtless dead, like her fool brudda. I need some air.

Creo *goes downstairs.*

Soldier One   See? See what I say?

Soldier Two   Shut up man!

Soldier One   No, I won't shut up. Why can't you admit it?

Soldier Two   To what?

Soldier One   That love does crazy shit to people.

Soldier Two   You call what you just saw, love?

Soldier One   In every meaning. Only love would make a son chat breeze to his dad like that. To mek him put his own life before his woman. Times when I wish I would give anything to have that, to do that.

Soldier Two   Look at me. Are we fam?

Soldier One   Of course.

Soldier Two   Would you put yer life before mine?

Soldier One (*offended*)   What kind of?

Soldier Two   Yes or no?

Soldier One   Yes, you fool.

Soldier Two   Good, cos I would for you. You ain't less than her, don't ever think that. Antigone's way is not the only way to love, you understand?

Scene Eight

Continuous from last scene.

Eamon *is with* **Tig** *in the cellar.*

Tig   What is wrong?

Eamon   It was nuttin.

Tig   I know it was nuttin.

Eamon   I just, didn't feel like it, alright?

Tig   You want to try again?

Eamon   In a minute.

I'm not some toy you can just wind up.

Tig   I know that.

Eamon   Because I'm Creo's son, ennit?

Tig   Eamon?

Eamon   Because I should know it all, like him? That I should be able to fling any gal and do it to her 24/7.

Tig   Not any gal, just me.

Eamon   Will you please get off that.

Tig   So, you turn man, good. I thought yer mum and her rubbish were gonna finish you off for good! You know she offered me dough.

Eamon   What?

Tig   For me to dash you. Leave Thebes and never come back.

Eamon   My mother?

Tig   Shoulda taken it, take it, run off, then laugh! Like it would make any difference. I knew you'd come back.

Eamon   Look, it's not going to happen, so just stop.

Tig   Eamon, I don't think you realise what is happening here?

Eamon   I know!

Tig   What is up wid you?

Eamon   You should have said yes.

Tig   What?

Eamon   From my mum, you should have taken the money. I could have waited outside the city walls.

Tig   Eamon?

Eamon   We could have gone, together. Be free, go anywhere!

Tig   I can't do that.

Eamon   Because you are just like him, my dad.

Tig   I am nothing like him.

Eamon   Yeah you are.

Tig   How can you say?

Eamon   Tight as anything, won't budge.

Tig   Calm yourself.

Eamon   I don't want to calm myself. How can I be calm, when all of this is going on?

Tig   Would you believe me if I say, I didn't want this.

Eamon   Tell him you were wrong.

Tig   No.

Eamon   That you are sorry.

Tig   I can't.

Eamon   Girl he's going to kill you.

Tig   And my brother?

Eamon   He's dead.

Tig   Someone has to speak for him.

Eamon   And that someone has to be you, right? Even though Eto' was wurtless and a half!

Tig   You say like I don't know.

Eamon   So why? Why are you doing this?

Tig   One of Creo's soldiers has this guy, owes him money. So, what does this guy go and do? Drags his girl round *Old Thebes* by her hair, offering her to anyone for a tenner, he did that all night, until his debt was paid. I don't understand this world, I never did. I don't know what Orrin, Eto' or Creo are fighting for.

Eamon   Have you ever thought about asking me what I am fighting for? Who I'm fighting for? You know, I don't think you ever loved me.

Tig   Well, you might as well go, if you think that.

Eamon   Sket!

Tig   Go on.

Eamon   Bitch.

Tig   Don't stop.

Eamon   Yer stupid bloody yat!

Tig   Yes, yer his son now. Go then, Ca this yat, this bitch plenty of oder man to see.

Eamon   I bet.

Tig   You!

Eamon   What?

Tig   You say. But you don't mean.

Eamon   When you were on your knees burying your dead brother, did you ever stop to think about us? What it would do to me if you were caught? Did you not feel a thing? Tell me! I think about you, all of the time. I lost a brother as well in case you forget. When Mekhi was killed, I found myself thinking of you, whilst he was lying there, my own brother, all dead up, I found myself thinking of you. At his funeral, all the time I was looking after my mum and dad, I found myself thinking of you. Coming here tonight, I found myself thinking of you. Ca I love you, girl. Not Tig, the sket, not Tig with the big mouth, who loves to talk and talk and talk about people's business all day, not Tig the inbred! Just Tig, the woman. I loved you from the first time I laid eyes. In the city, all those guys, wanted to rush you, I thought; yer too good for that. Still are. There's more to it than just sexing each other, there has to be, yeah? There has to be more than this, tell me I'm worth it.

Tig   Say that again.

Eamon   What bit?

Tig   The whole bit. All of it. (*Kisses his forehead.*) Boy, you are the most craziest brudda I know. My boy. My sweet boy.

Eamon   But you're still going to go through aren't you?

Tig   I have to.

Eamon   No you don't.

Tig   Eamon please, don't make this harder than it is. Don't make me question it any more than I already have. Please, I beg you. Now please put your face back, your beautiful smiling face. Smile at me, smile, come on! (*He smiles.*) Thank you. Lie down with me.

Eamon   Tig, I told you, I don't think I can . . .

Tig   And now I'm telling you, it don't matter. Lie with me.

Tig *takes his hand, they lie down together and embrace. Two of the* **Soldiers** *enter and drag* **Tig** *away.*

Eamon   Let her go! I said leave her yeah! Do you know who I am? I said, do you know?

The **Soldiers** *ignore* **Eamon***'s cries as they continue to drag* **Tig** *away.* **Eamon** *holds his head in his hands as he cries.*

Eunice *enters and pulls him up.*

Eunice   What are you doing? I asked you a question, boy, what do you think this is? You do not cry in front of them, in front of anyone! Dry your eyes now. Dry your eyes! you are Creo's son, the next in line to take over, are you trying to shame him or what?

Eamon   I don't care.

Eunice   Well you had better start.

Eamon   Mum, just leave me, yeah!

Eunice   See this here, and everything else, it will be yours boy.

Eamon   I don't want it.

Eunice   Gwan home and fix up.

Eamon   I don't think you heard me.

Eunice   Hard not to, seeing as I am standing right by you.

Eamon   You offered her money, Mum.

Eunice   I offered her a chance.

Eamon   Is there still time?

Eunice   What?

Eamon   For her to go?

Eunice   Son?

Eamon   She'll say yes, I'll make her, then she'll go.

Eunice   And what about you?

Eamon   Me?

Eunice   What are you going to do?

Eamon   Nothing, I'm safe. As long as she is alright. I will do what you want, marry whoever you want me to, have a whole heap of grandkids for you, if that is what it takes, but I'm begging you let her live, please!

Eunice   Bwoi, don't tek me for an idiot, yeah? The minute she tek one foot outside the city walls, you are going to be following after her, like you always do.

Eamon   She my girl.

Eunice   Was your girl!

Eamon   Mum, just give her the money yeah?

Eunice   She wouldn't take it, she still wouldn't, you know why? Because she is not right in the head like the rest of her disgusting family. She is not normal.

Eamon   I don't care about that, I don't business.

Eunice   Now, you sound like yer father.

Eamon   No.

Eunice   Don't wanna listen, just worry about yourself.

Eamon   Well leave us if you're so unhappy, leave us both.

Eunice   Did I say I was unhappy? I made my choice long ago.

Eamon   Mum, please?

Eunice   Don't beg. Get a grip. You are . . .

Eamon   Creo's son!

Eunice   That's right! Now you have a name and a kingdom to uphold. Man up!

Eamon   Fuck the kingdom.

Eunice   You do not talk to me so.

Eamon   And fuck my name cos I don't care.

Eunice   Eamon?

Eamon   You don't hear me say, I don't care.

Eunice   What you may or not care about, or even what you think about anything is irrelevant. Don't you understand that by now? Or did I just spend the last eighteen years raising a fool for a son? Well, which is it?

Eamon   Mum?

Eunice   Mum, what?

Eamon   Help me man.

Eunice   I will slap those tears out of your eyes in a minute, dry them!

Eamon *dries his eyes.*

Eunice   She defied your father, she has to pay. Now come move yourself.

Eunice *goes to leave.*

Eunice (*calls*)   Eamon?

Eamon *follows his mother.*

Scene Nine

Continuous from scene before.

Tig *is brought back into the VIP area.*

Tig   If Creo wants to dead me, why don't he just get on with it? Let me enjoy my last night in peace man. You think I don't know, what he has planned for me? Tell him to go bring himself.

Soldier One   So you can die the hero!

Tig   I ain't no hero, I jus do what's right.

Soldier One   Hear yourself, you can't wait, can you? You can't wait to die, be a hero.

Soldier Two   Sick in the head like the rest of your family.

Tig   Listen yeah, as soon as one of you dead me, you've got all your years left to diss me. At least they know.

Soldier One   Who?

Tig   The people, innit?

Soldier Three   Know what?

Tig   That I have been judged unfairly. They will know.

Soldier One   They will also know there was no helping you, not ever, not once!

Soldier Two   Not with your father's mad up blood in you.

Tig   Well carry on, don't stop. Keep rubbing that salt. Tell me more about my crazy blind dad! So stupid, he couldn't see, couldn't feel he was sexing up his own mudda! That all he's done is curse me with crazy sick madness! Tell me! Tell me that I'm going down and it might as well be his own hand that's dragging me there!

Creo *enters.*

Soldier Two   You knew what you were doing, you knew what would happen. Yer summin girl, you really are, but crazy ain't it.

Tig   How can I not be, if I got no one who's gonna cry for me. Cos this is my last day.

Creo   Girl, I go give you one last chance, yeah? One! Enough with the foolishness, say yer sorry, leave your wurtless brother where he is.

Tig   And say no more?

Creo   We deal or what?

Tig   Take me to my hole. I will have my fam waiting for me, my real fam!

Creo   Yeah girl they're waiting. Nuttin but a bunch of inbreds, all waiting for you in inbred heaven!

Tig   My brother, my beautiful brother! Who I died for. When you left him out there to the dogs, do you think I had a choice? If this was my man or husband we're talking about, I might have had a choice. Cos I could always have another kid, I could always find me a new man. How am I supposed to find me a new brother, when my mum and dad are in the ground? Look up to you as a brother? Can you imagine, cos I know I can't. No matter what you might think, I know my conscience is clear. In fact I know already what you are thinking. I have broken the law, your law, gone and committed a heinous act. You make me laugh that you believe that shit. That I deserve this. If I do, fair enough, we will see what the afterlife has for me. But you're more guilty than me, Creo, know that.

Soldier Three   She don't stop.

Soldier Two   As wild as ever.

Tig   I won't forget, the whole of *Thebes* won't forget.

The guards appear.

Creo (*waits*)   What are you waiting for, rain?

Tig   Yes, you heard the man! Mister big man!

Creo   Now!

Tig   Come take me!

The guards take **Tig** *away.*

Creo   I want drink!

Creo *goes to the bar.*

Soldier Two   Hey.

Soldier One   Hey what?

Soldier Two   Don't give us that look.

Soldier One   What look?

Soldier Two   That look!

Soldier One   Brer mad.

Soldier Two   That look that makes you think you should tell Creo how wrong he is about killing her.

Soldier One   I wasn't.

Soldier Two   Well that's alright then.

Soldier One   But if I was?

Soldier Two   You see?

Soldier One   Hold up.

Soldier Three   Fool ain't the word.

Soldier One   All I'm saying is.

Soldier Two   Stop saying. Right now.

Soldier Two   Tig had it coming.

Soldier Three   He tried to reach, she dashed him.

Soldier One   Check this brer! Like he's on it now.

Soldier Two   He's right. Done deal.

Soldier Three   By the way it's a crow.

Soldier Two   How you know?

Soldier Three   Found a picture, it look just like the other one I had, crow!

Soldier   Nice but wass it mean?

Lights on **Tig** *alone in the cellar. She looks and stares up at the
CCTV overhead.*

Tig   You're jokers and a half, Did you know that? You
nuttin but bastards, the lot of yer, sick idle bastards! Are you
having fun? Having a good time at the way we are carrying
on? Who's displeasing you the most right now, Creo or me?
Or do you not even care? You can't, you can't care. You
would have done something by now, not just me, but
everyone, you can see what's going on, how people are
living. You don't care, so why should I business about you?
Cos I don't. I didn't do it in your name, let's make that clear.
I am of my own mind, I did it for me, not because you would
let me go otherwise, you'd make Creo see, before it's too late,
then you would let me go, let me get on with my life, you
would! You would. Wouldn't you? Waiting? Why? Why me,
why do I have to die as well? My mum and dad weren't
enough for you, so you took my brothers, was that supposed
to be funny, rub my nose in it? So what am I, for good
measure? Probably just as well cos if Creo let me go, I would
have gone after you lot as well, believe me, I would gone to
town on you, tell everyone how it is, our beloved gods!
Who's up next in the firing line, Esme? She's not as weak as
you think. She'll fight you. Dead me, and I promise you she
will fight. Them people, they are tougher than you think.
They will see the light soon enough one day. And when they
do, yer done.

Tyrese *enters, being led in by a young boy.* **Creo** *returns from
the bar.*

Creo   Tyrese! You dat? Come on in, you wurtless old fart!

Tyrese   Look pon me now Creo, how one can see for two.
Boy, set me down here.

Creo   Man, are you a sight.

Tyrese   Sight? You mek joke?

Creo   To you? Nuh man, no, never! I'm glad yer here, man.

Tyrese   You called, so I come.

Creo   You have to help me.

Tyrese   I know. That is the only why I came.

Creo   Back in the day, you was a soldier, you saw shit, you did shit, you know what it means to stand tall, get respect, lay down the law on people.

Tyrese   I did.

Creo   Everything I do, I learn from brers like you, you understand, yeah?

Tyrese   I do.

Creo   You lose your eyes for what you believe.

Tyrese   I did.

Creo   Well help me out here, cos right now, I have nothing but pussies and good fer nuttin skets telling me how I should handle myself, my business! Like I'm wrong all of the time. That I must answer to them. (*Points to the cameras.*) I rules *Thebes,* I am the king, how can I be wrong, tell me, in fact, actually, don't tell me, tell them, tell all of them!

Tyrese   I will. Him the king.

Creo   Yes! Thank you! So, wat you have for me old man? What you have for me today?

Tyrese   Well that depends.

Creo   On what?

Tyrese   On whether you are going to listen?

Creo   Don't I always listen to you? Have I ever not done as you have said? You are General Tyrese! There is no need to doubt me.

Tyrese   No, you've always listened, heard me out, I give you that.

Creo   We is fam! I owe you hundred times over.

Tyrese   Good, so listen up, and listen good, because what I have to say is important.

Creo   What is it that you have to say?

Tyrese   That you are in deep shit.

Creo   Don't come here telling me that, Tyrese, please. I told you I have enough people tonight telling me that. That is not why you are here, at least I hope not. What else do your visions have for me? What can you see? Look ahead man, in years to come. Tell me Thebes is thriving. Tell me my boy is on the throne, doing good. Tell me all that, I want to hear.

Tyrese   Creo, you ask me to look, so I look. But I heard nothing, I saw nothing but screams and cries. The sound of Thebes, old and new tearing its way at each other like animals.

Creo   Is it?

Tyrese   Rivers of blood mi tell yu.

Creo   I had to ask, innit?

Tyrese   The people turning on each other, clawing at each other.

Creo   Tyrese, Tyrese man, I keep telling you, you have to cut down on the skunk man. You smoke it like it is going out of fashion.

Tyrese   Hear me.

Creo   Hear what?

Tyrese   Clawing away!

Creo   Yes, a whole heap of madness going on, what about my son? He's dealing with this, this madness that you are going wid? Well is he, or isn't he? Tyrese? Hello? Now would be an appropriate time for you to say summin? So say summin?

Tyrese   You do not see?

Creo   Sorry. No.

Tyrese   The sign?

Creo   What sign, man? For fu . . .

Tyrese   That you are responsible for all of this. All of this.

Creo   All of that! It hasn't happened yet.

Tyrese   All from the stain from the body of Orrin.

Creo   Here it comes, I knew it. Bloody knew it. You're letting me down, Tyrese, you are letting me down big style. I am on top of this?

Tyrese   Creo, all men make mistakes.

Creo   Not me.

Tyrese   It is alright.

Creo   Not for me.

Tyrese   To make amends.

Creo   Say?

Tyrese   Redemption. To show your people you are full of good will.

Creo   Tell me summin, did you ever show your enemies good will?

Tyrese   Me?

Creo   Yes man, who else?

Tyrese   Not even once.

Creo   So, why should I?

Tyrese   Because I am no longer a king. Because I am sitting here with two holes in my head, where my eyes used to be.

Creo   We all make mistakes, but that don't have to mean that I must make your kind.

Tyrese   Creo?

Creo   Is that it? Cos if it is, you can go.

Tyrese   What is it that you want?

Creo   Tell me about *Thebes*, tell me what a beautiful and powerful city it will come to be. None of this 'rivers of blood', chaos on the streets crap. Tell me about my son.

Tyrese   Gone.

Creo   Gone? Gone where?

Tyrese   That is what I am trying to tell you, gone.

Creo   What kind of future is this?

Tyrese   The future you asked for.

Creo   Asked for? The future I want is the future I want. That I pay for.

Tyrese   It does not work like that.

Creo   It does now. You need to revise a few things. Now, you tell me about my son. Tell me how strong he is. How many sons does he have? How beautiful is his wife? Come on old man, give it up.

Tyrese   Ask yourself, what is the point in killing a man who is dead already? You have to change your mind on this.

Creo   I do not have to do anything.

Tyrese   You have heard me before, hear me now.

Creo   Hear what? Another hustle? You are always trying to shake me down, innit Tyrese, and like a fool I listen, ca it put a smile on my face. You really think this is going to trick me into burying Orrin? No, Nossir!

Tyrese   I thought you'd be wise.

Creo   I am wise.

Tyrese   Then use it, for all of its worth.

Creo   And find myself bruc in the process?

Tyrese   You already are boy, if you keep thinking like that.

Creo   Look, it ain't on my agenda to have a quarrel with a crazy old man.

Tyrese   Crazy? A few seconds ago I was a general.

Creo   A few seconds ago, you hadn't opened your mouth.

Tyrese   You believe that I am crazy now?

Creo   I believe any man who sees what you see, do what you do, wants paying.

Tyrese   And I believe all kings are fools!

Creo   Mind yourself, you don't chat back, you don't talk like that, not to me!

Tyrese   Big man!

Creo   Only man!

Tyrese   I saved this city as well, I didn't hide behind my soldiers like you, I fought, I killed, l lost my eyes.

Creo   I don't deny your role, you tell the future good and all that. But you ain't got the front, let alone the strength, not to go out and sell your gift. The will, for that matter, not to let yourself be swayed outta corruption. Is it?

Tyrese   I think you had better stop right there.

Creo   I stop when I want.

Tyrese   You wanna know what I see in store for you? Your future? I thought not.

Creo   Wrong again, old man. You just caught me, that is all. So come on then, bring it, tell me about my future. Just don't expect to be paid for this.

Tyrese   You cannot change it, you cannot redeem it.

Creo   You think? You think I don't know? Nothing you, or them (*to the* **Soldiers**) or them (*points to the cameras*) can make me change, nothing! The girl is going to die!

Tyrese   Fine, just be sure that you will pay for her life and for the life of yer bwoi! All this, just to put some girl through a living death, insulting our gods in the process.

Creo *laughs. He waves to the cameras in a dismissive manner.*

Tyrese   This is no way to treat the dead, that is what they telling me to tell you. If you don't stop this, Creo, if you don't stop this now, they unleash a whole heap of fury on your arse! You still thinking it's just noise I chat? How can you expect them people to follow you, to love you, to die for you, when you will not grant one of the purest human needs, to bury the dead, they will move against you, every single one of them. Are you going to throw them all into a dark hole? You might as well throw yourself, you and your own blasted stubbornness. This bad bwoi act can only last so far, believe me, I know.

Creo   Who are you calling a boy?

Tyrese   But those who do not listen must feel, help me up. Where are you boy?

Boy   Here, sir.

Tyrese   Then come! We will leave our king, to think, if he have any good sense left in him? If you uses the time to find his tongue and use it wisely! He can start by apologising to me, for calling me a fool.

The **Boy** *leads* **Tyrese** *away.*

Creo *looks up at the cameras.*

Creo   Well? Come on then, what do you have to say, show me what you've got? Don't use Tyrese, or my boy, or anyone else to say what you feel, tell me yourself. Am I the king or not? Tell me you don't approve, say, tell, show? Waiting! Just as I thought, there nuttin there, no one's there, no one's there! See me I got what I want, by myself, not you, me! I made things happen, I rise up myself to rule you hear me? I got nuttin from you, I don't need you. So, if you're go chat, then chat now to me, come on, what you have for me?

Creo *eyes his* **Soldiers**.

Creo   Yeah? What? You are just going to stand there and say nothing?

Soldier Three   What do you want us to say?

Creo   Just don't chat no lyrics to me about gods.

Soldier Two   Alright, but I have never known Tyrese to lie, or any one of his visions not to come true.

Creo   Maybe that's his trick.

Soldier Two   Say?

Creo   He does a good talk of what is going to happen, somehow, whether we like it or not, we have a way making sure it does happen.

Soldier Two   So you reject what he says.

Creo   Tell me summin, if they (*points at cameras*) are so knowing, as Tyrese says, why don't they say summin, why don't they make their move?

Soldier Two   Maybe they did. Maybe you're right the gods ain't there, but in here! (*Taps his head.*) Listen to yourself doubting yourself. That's where the power lies, man, real power.

Creo   I'm supposed to go back on my word.

Soldier Two   You are supposed to do what you must.

Creo   Which is what?

Soldier Two   You know what.

Let Tig cover her brother.

Creo   As simple as that?

Soldier Two   Alright if you can't.

Creo   Can't, who said I can't? I didn't say I can't, are you saying I can't?

Soldier Two   You don't have much time here.

Creo   Alright, I'm going. I may be harsh, but I'm fair.

Soldier Three   You should do this yourself, fam. Don't trust anyone else to do this. Now, man!

Creo   I'm going, I'm going. Bring me soldiers to meet me at the quarry, tell them to bring shovels and shit. I want to pull her out of there myself. Now!

Soldier Two (*on his phone*)   On it!

Creo *goes, followed by his* **Soldiers**.

Scene Ten

A main road. Continuous from previous scene.

Eamon *runs on with* **Tig**. *They have made it to the busy main road. They stand on the edge, about to cross.*

Tig   OMG!

Who taught you to fight like that?

Eamon   Who do you think?

Tig   You're his son alright, no doubt.

Eamon   I'm me, Tig. That's all I can be. Funny, but if this was different circumstances, he woulda been proud of me, beating up on four of his soldiers like that.

Tig   I counted three.

Eamon   Three, four, I gave them licks!

Eamon   I couldn't stand away and let them bury you alive.

Tig   He will come for us.

Eamon   Shush.

Tig   He won't stop looking, you know that.

Eamon   He will have to find us.

Tig   You think he won't?

Eamon   Only if the whole begins and ends with Thebes.

Tig   So, what now then?

Eamon   We go.

Tig   Go where?

Eamon   Anywhere we want, we're free.

Tig   You might be.

Eamon   You're not in the cellar no more.

Tig   I didn't do this because I wanted to escape, Eamon.

I didn't do this to start looking over my shoulder, that is no life for me.

Eamon   But you do want to die.

Tig   I want peace.

Eamon   You think I want that life as well? Why you think I'm running?

I can't go back.

Tig   Neither can I.

Eamon   We had better go then.

Tig   Eamon?

Eamon   Did you not hear what I had just said? We had better go.

Eamon *clasps her hand.*

Tig *kisses him.*

Creo *and the* **Soldiers** *enter.*

They both run out onto the road. Lights down, sound of a vehicle slamming into them.

Creo *kneels down sobbing at the sight of the two bodies. He removes his jacket and attempts to cover them both with it.*

The **Three Soldiers** *return to the VIP area.* **Soldier Two** *gets a text.*

Soldier Two   I got it.

Soldier Three   Say?

Soldier Two   When you got more than one crow, a whole heap of them, they called a murder. 'A murder of crows.' Two crows by themselves is attempted murder.

Soldier Three   All that time for that?

Soldier Two   Believe.

Soldier One   I tell yer.

Soldier Two   Don't start.

Soldier One   Alright I won't.

Soldier Two   Best not.

Soldier One   See me shutting up.

Soldier Three   What?

Soldier One   He what, what?

Soldier Three   What is it that you want to say?

Soldier Two   What, you as well?

Soldier Three   You started, you may as well finish.

Soldier One   Alright, what I was about to say yeah, was no matter who you follow religious wise, God is God.

Soldier Three   Yeah?

Soldier One   His word, his will, end of. Discussion.

Soldier Three   Yeah, we know!

Soldier One   I know you know.

Soldier Three   I thought you say God is in us.

Soldier One   That's what I mean, go against what you know to be right and you'll find out. We make our own choices, and out of that, our fate. God made us this way. He can't undo it. Creo made his choice to bling himself up. Rise up from being a soldier, so he can lead us all. He decided to throw his own niece into a hole. Forgive me for speaking out of turn but he only has himself to blame.

Soldier Two   What you say?

Soldier Three   Shank this fool!

Soldier One   Feeling brave now *Sentry!* Come on then, shank me!

Soldier Two   Not us, not here, you understand?

Soldier One   How much you want bet Creo wouldn't give up everything he has, even his life if he could change things now. How much you want bet? (*Clocks their faces.*) Good call. Cos there is no way I would make that kind of bet now.

Soldier Three   Just keep it quiet.

Soldier One   All I am saying.

Soldier Two   Is this you keeping quiet?

Soldier Three   You want die for real? Do yourself a favour and shut up.

Soldier One   Doubt it all we like.

Soldier Three   We are not listening to you.

Soldier Two   Can't you tell?

Soldier One   Wisdom lies in what we know what it means to be right. Creon left it too late.

Soldier Two   You think?

The **Soldiers** *leave.*

Scene Twelve

An hour later.

Creo *faces* **Eunice.**

Creo   What?

Eunice   What do you want me to say?

Creo   Come on girl.

Eunice   Controlled as ever.

Creo   Is that a joke?

Eunice   Like I have got the energy for jokes.

Creo   We need to work out what are going to do?

Eunice   Do?

Creo   What to say and that?

Eunice   To who, Creo?

Creo   The people, Thebes.

Eunice   Yes, yes of course, it's king and queen time, put our reasonable faces on.

Creo   We don't have a choice.

Eunice   Oh but I do, Creo. I have a choice.

Creo   Blame me? Is that it?

Eunice   Everything is about you, the way you want.

Creo   But you want blame me? Right or wrong? Well go on, do what you feel.

Eunice   I told you not to let him get mixed up with her, how many times did I tell you?

Creo   Is that it, is that all you have to cuss me with, Eunice? Girl, you slipping.

Eunice   Don't make fun of me.

Creo   Girl, you are on a planet far away if you think I am doing that.

Eunice   You didn't care that she was an inbred. All you cared about was that she had a fine arse on her.

Creo   What?

Eunice   That she could move her batty like so.

Creo (*to cameras*)   Oh gods come on, help me out here!

Eunice   That's all you cared about.

Creo   Yes Eunice, that must be it.

Eunice   That she wanted yer boy, you got off on that. Ca yer too old. An inbred Creo, inbred, I told you.

Creo   And I told you to stop fussing after him, telling him this, telling him that, from the time he could crawl. Nothing was right, everything he did was wrong. Him not a bwoi, him a man, but you wouldn't stop. He went wid that crazy gal cos of you not because of me. Him come crying to me, begging me to free his woman, my son, chatting to me like some gal. You did that, bloody you, so don't come into my face playing the saint.

Eunice   If I fussed, it was because I had to. He was your son, your heir. There was no normal life for him. I didn't want this for him.

Creo   Bullshit.

Eunice   I did not.

Creo   Did I ever hear you complain when I kept yer arse in gold? You *Old Thebes skank!*

Eunice *removes her jewellery and throws them.*

Eunice   You want them back, take them, take them!

Creo   Boy dead and we're still fighting over him.

Eunice *goes to leave.*

Creo   You go tell me what I have to do? Eunice? Eunice? Tell me what I have to do, tell me, cos I don't get it, cos I don't know, this is all I know, this is all I do, tell me what you need from me, what do I have to do to make you forgive me, tell me . . .

Eunice (*in a rage*)   **NOTHING!** You took everything that was good about him, killed him inside you . . . you killed my son . . . you killed him . . . there is . . . **NOTHING!**

Eunice *goes.* **Creo** *sits alone.*

The following action takes back to the same spot where the play began. Lights indicate a passage of time, seven years in fact. **Creo**, *is older, sadder, and broken. He takes a bottle out of a plastic carrier bag and lies down.*

Esme *enters. She brings him a jacket and covers* **Creo** *and offers him a hot drink.*

Lights down.